The Windhorse

The Windhorse

POEMS OF ILLUMINATION

Ayn Cates Sullivan, Ph.D.

Order this book online at www.trafford.com
or email orders@trafford.com
Most Trafford titles are also available at major online book retailers.

Revised 1ST Edition

© Copyright 2012 Ayn Cates Sullivan, Ph.D.

Artwork by Gwen Cates

Printed in the United States of America.

ISBN: 978-1-4669-5231-7 (sc)
ISBN: 978-1-4669-5230-0 (e)

Trafford rev. 08/13/2012

 www.trafford.com

North America & international
toll-free: 1 888 232 4444 (USA & Canada)
phone: 250 383 6864 ♦ fax: 812 355 4082

Contents

J Catte

This book is dedicated
to my Beloved John Patrick Sullivan
who rides with me on the Windhorse,
for with him all things are possible.

Love Song

I have been knocking on all the doors
In the village looking for you
And have been exploring all the stars in heaven
Calling your name.
I wish to be a torchbearer for your infinite flame.
Please expose me to your inner sun
So that I may be illuminated by you;
Fill me with your grace
So that I may be a light upon this world.
I am a flute waiting to be played by you.
Please use me
In your next love song.

May I Play Again

I wish to free all that waits within me to be born.
May my limitations be washed away
By a silent river.
May I play again
As a child in the ebbing and flowing
Currents of existence.
I open my mouth to sing,
Yet feel ashamed for an instant.
Who am I to have such a great longing?
Please forgive me
But I wish to write this opera.
I want to know my own life
And how to move with it.
I yearn to know God's immensity
And how to mirror it
Without shattering.
I sense that where I am closed and tight
I am yet untrue.
I want to unfurl
So that no blossom within me
Is fruitless or withered
And no song is left unsung.

If Light Can Speak

The Light came to visit me and spoke—
If light can speak—
It was more of a song
That blew through my hair
The way starlight weaves its way into the night.
It understood that the heart already knows
And so it is time to listen
In a new way
One not so fraught with concern
Because things have a way of continuing.
The daffodil does not despair
When the summer sun begins to shine
And she withers,
For she will come again
And perfume the garden
Yet another time.
This is a never ending journey
And yet cycles do mark passages
Set up so we can learn
And grow like a forest
Filled with seeds
Awaiting the right timing
For our birth.

A Sunflower

Tonight I feel like ripening
Until I am real.
I am tired of trying
To get it right.
I'd rather just blossom
Like a sunflower
And turn my face
Towards the sun.
God likes what
Is real and true.
He can reach for you then
And set your heart a blaze.
A flame helps us all
See in the darkness.

Tapestry

The sea is blacker than the night.
Waves push and suck the gray stones.
The wind threads cool and warm air
Like a tapestry through the wild lands.
A white sea bird carried by the breeze
Surrenders beneath the swelling silver stars.
The waxing white moon casts a pearly light
Illuminating a blazing chalice
On the absence of the night.

The Chasm of Self

There are nights when I love the darkness
And step out into the timeless universe
Placing a foot on one star after another

Carefully as a child
Quivering on the mossy rocks
Balancing and breathing
As she crosses a roaring river.

The stars have some substance
But the black spaces in between
Are as empty and mysterious
As a lake with no known depth.

I wonder what lurks there
In that chasm of self?
Perhaps our light has been stored away
With all the mythical creatures

And in that darkness
We may find the potentiality of all that exists.
I suspect we may also encounter
What dissolves us.

That mysterious blackness
Is why I prefer to step
On one star after another.

Sensing You

When I find you
Don't allow me
To bind you to image
Or utterance
I would rather sense you
As I ripen
Into what is real.

Eternal Flame

At first I thought you were a trespasser.
Go away, I said. I am married.
But the feeling continued to grow
Catching my heart on fire
With an eternal flame.
I thought it was you, I said.
There was only silence
As the heat raced up and down my spine
Like a garden snake on warm stones.
I love you! I told my husband.
He smiled and kissed me.
The feeling did not change.
I love you! I told my son.
He snuggled up close to my chest.
Still the feeling did not change.
I told my inner self that I loved her too.
A warmth as strong as a passing comet
Flooded each and every cell in my body,
Light bounced off my organs
And healed my tissues,
But the feeling did not change.
It is not about someone else, is it?
I asked the feeling.
Joy swept through me.
This is how the Beloved speaks.

I looked outside and saw light resting
In the leaves of the Peppertrees.
Roses beneath them shared perfume
With the gentle breeze.
The birds sang together
In a harmonious chorus.
These things are always here for us.
It is so simple
That we forget the truth.
Closing my eyes I went within
And saw an internal light,
Smelled an inner sweetness,
Heard the heart beating
In rhythm with all that exists.
We are not separate at any moment
But part of a wholeness
That is eternal.

Pearl

Luminous lights kiss my form.
I'm held in the arms of creation.
I cease to care
About who I've been
Or what I've done.
It is meaningless
In the grand scheme of things
For who I am is not my content
Who I am
Is a luminosity,
A bright effervescent
Living pearl.

Singing with Existence

The crickets called me out one night.
Their song was so incredulous
That I had to listen
Until I became one with their song.
If you listen at night you will hear it too.
Their rhythm links us to the night wind
That enlivens us with dreams.
You see, when you really listen to their chorus
Your own song awakens within you
And you can't help it—
You start dancing like a madman
But really you are singing with existence.
If you don't let people's comments disturb you
You can start dancing too
And the dust under your feet
Will reveal patterns that only mystics know.
You realize that whatever force
Moves your arms and legs
With such a wild frenzy,
Or graceful ease,
Loves you so much
That if you really got it
Your mind would explode
Into a thousand suns
And you would see yourself
As you are—
Dancing in the moonlight
To the songs of crickets.

Arising

When we arise early in the morning
As the sun rises over the rocky peaks of the mountains
Or sends its light across the vast oceans,
We have a moment
In which we can remember
The sun or brilliant star
That resides within our own being.
In fifteen billion years
This star has remained unchanged.
One incarnation after another,
The gold simply reveals
The genius of life.

From The Heart

I hear my husband awaken.
He has become as familiar
As the sun to me.
His presence is as constant.
We share our inner worlds and nod
As if we understand one another.
But there is always a great mystery
Inside a person that can never
Be known by the mind.
You see, there are some places
That are reserved for the heart
And when you try to speak
With the lips of the heart
You tend to mumble or hum
Or even sing and sometimes
A great poem bursts forth,
But then you realize
You forgot to write it down.
It is that way with the heart.
Things simply are
And that is enough.
My marriage is of the heart
So there is no need to speak
Except that it can be fun
To explore life together like children
Finding starfish in the sand.

Ancient Thread

The snow weaves a pattern of light in the mist.
This is an ancient thread.
If you touch a snowflake it melts
And if you close your eyes you also disappear
Into the heart of the mountains
Where there are formless caves
And treasures beyond description.
When you touch the ancient thread
It leads you home
With your heart pumping so furiously
That you may need to start singing
Because it is so magnificent.
This is what happens to the birds
At sunrise when they feel
The rays of light warming their breasts
And want to share
What joy life is!
They cannot keep it to themselves
And so they announce
The beauty of the world with their songs
Harmonizing with each other
Like the players in an orchestra
As a symphony begins.
Oh world, you are such a glimmering jewel.

At times my eyesight has become dusty
And I have not seen clearly.
Today I see you are unchanging.
The snow weaves a pattern of light in the mist.
This is an ancient thread
Which we can follow Home.

Fire

I feel fires in the mountains
Sizzling and snapping around the feet of trees.
The animals are fleeing
Past houses and roads
Into some unknown territory.
What can I do but follow them?
Perhaps it takes a blaze to make us shift
When all seems so familiar.
The fire has its own ideas
As it leaps and devours what it wishes,
Cleansing in harmony with the elements
In a way difficult to grasp.
What can we do but bow down
To the temporary nature of things?
The truth is that life is always changing.
Soon we will see new growth where we walk
Through fields greening and healing
As the ocean mist sends its morning balm.
The skeletons of trees will topple
Under the new growth of springtime flowers.
The change is beautiful if you can embrace
Both the morning glories and the charred remains
That makes such rich fertilizer.
The land is being purified
So there is more room for light,
New spaces for us to grow into
And less to carry home.

The Living Wind

Is it the Light that lives life through me?
Or do I live life through God?
Or are we simply friends
Playing in the universe together?

Maybe as we align with the earth,
The rain and the breath of the living wind
We sprout like young seeds
In the springtime sun.

The Beloved

How long can we truly stand being in the light?
How long must the bird sing until we hear her?
The distant hum of traffic reminds us of what is elsewhere,
The busyness we engage in when we forget
How precious each moment truly is:

Every breath is a gift
Still we cry and suffer
Saying we do not know the divine.
How can we not know
That we are as fully immersed in the Beloved
As a Humpbacked whale is in the ocean?
How can we not know what we already are?

The emptiness of the moment
Reveals an orchestra of aliveness:
All of our hearts beat together
Yet each of us peer at the world
Through a different pair of spectacles:
Some examining books, others feeling
Or loving, hating or laughing
According to our true nature.

The Beloved rejects no one,
For there is nothing that can be rejected.
We can choose to block
The storehouse of abundance.
We can choose to say no
To our gifts, talents and dreams.
But why stay small?

Why suffer when there is no such thing as suffering?
There is only a momentary forgetting of the truth—
Of essential love and support
For eternal presence is with us as we live
And die and live again
In each and every moment.

The Beloved is here,
Will you turn him away
Or turn towards him
With open arms?

Eclipsed

Everything I say, write or paint
Can be eclipsed by your Presence.
We spend time naming things
Yet you take the words back
Into the great silence.
I want to love all of creation
As it is right now.
This small form is breaking
Beneath your magnitude.
Please hold me
While you are writing.

Cosmic Pulse

At dusk the remaining radiance
Casts tints of rose and lilac
Onto this small form
And across the sweep of fields.
Astride my white mare
I gaze eastward towards the mountains
That reach up towards the heavens
Alive with galaxies and mysteries.
This body and mind dissolve
Into the cosmic pulse
Of what is real.
Light begins to stream
Through a diamond opening
In my burning forehead.
A hot and luminous thread of liquid light
Spreads through my spine
And my horse gives a shudder
Before bending her head to graze
On the ripening grasses.
There is no separation
Between myself and the mare
Or the plants being plucked
And ground into liquid green.
I feel like I am making love
With an intelligence

Greater than I,
Of which I am still a part,
That loves all things with tenderness and ease.
The mare is ready for home now
And so we set off at a gallop
Towards a light in the distance.
I lay the reins upon her neck
And reaching towards the stars
I am carried safely home.

For A While

When a soul attunes with you
And likes you enough to stay
You can be invited to become a mother
For a while.

It can happen when you are simply
Walking down the street
Just humming
Thinking about life.

The illusion may become complete
If you think the baby is yours,
Nothing is ours forever.

The truth is much more beautiful.
The mother is loved so much
That we can become the chosen one
For a while.

The Tiny Grasses

Beloved Creator
I Love You
And Creatures Of All Shapes And Sizes
May I Remember To Love The Small Things
The Tiny Grasses
The Details Of The Flowers
The Smiles On Children's Lips
And Observe That The Whole World
Is Supported In Its Unfolding

My Daughter Dreaming
Her Self Into Being

I want to tell you about the day I balanced
On the ridge of a blue mountain
And my daughter, not yet born, decided to visit.
In that moment the land and I were as thin
And bare as the spine of a wild boar,
But all things that feel empty seek to be filled.
A wisp of a cloud joined us and I began to laugh with delight.
That was the thought of my daughter
Dreaming her self into being.
She came to me as a spark from a daytime star
That no one can see but a mother.
Dazzled by a mirror-like sun
I could see my own imp-like face in her
The past and the future stilled into one moment
Like a blue diamond.
She entered my body as a faint rumbling
The way a herd of deer enter a forest
And then consume it.
When I gave birth to her
We both took a place in this world together for a time.
These millions of seconds with her
Are the dearest of pearls.

Intimacy

I'll love you
All the way to God
But not in the way that you expect,
Not in the way you hoped.
I give you these kisses
To help you fall in love
With yourself
So you can see your own beauty
And trust yourself enough
To unfurl like an illuminated fern
In the sunlight
Of your own making.

Love Is Enough

I looked into the baby's eyes
And saw the world of spirit still there.
An angel stood over her
And seemed surprised that I saw him.
He put his finger to his lips
Saying, "Hush, we don't talk of such things here
Because if we did you wouldn't forget
And find out everything you are here to learn."
So I closed my eyes just feeling her essence,
Blue and undisturbed in the peacefulness of the moment.
Holding her reminded me that to simply be here
And love one another is quite enough.
Nothing more is required.
The angel looked at me and smiled
Before dispersing into light.

A Lilac Rose

Do not touch my soul
There are furies in there
Who protect the gems and diamonds
That reside deep within me.

Do not touch my soul
Even though she is enchanting
And beautiful to behold
For the moment you touch her
You are lost forever.

Do not touch my soul
For the juice of creation
Resides within her
And she is too powerful to gaze upon
And keep your mind.

Do not touch my soul
Because she cares deeply
For all things and if you touch her
You will realize where you
Have stopped caring for the world
And you will weep until rivers
Come to dry your eyes.

Do not touch my soul
Because she is as hot as a razor in the desert
And she knows how to defend herself,
Though mostly she just slips away
Before anyone notices her.

Do not touch my soul
Until you have been purified
By the fires of consciousness
And you have come to know
Your True Self.

Do not touch my soul
Until you are ready to gaze upon the Beloved
And allow your heart to crack open
Ten thousand times.

Do not touch my soul
Unless the fingers of your soul
Decide to spontaneously and gently
Grasp the fingers of my soul
In friendship and love.

Do not touch my soul
Until the world is ready
For this moment
For all things will change:
Night will be day
And day will be night.

Do not touch my soul
Until the dove gives you a lilac rose
As a sign that she is ready
And then heaven upon heaven
The Elysium fields will reveal themselves
And paradise is yours.

Do not touch my soul
Until you are ready
To be touched
And broken
And loved.

Listen

Finally you've forgiven yourself enough
To be God's instrument.
Any time you stop humming
And begin to fall
Through a crack
Listen with your inner ear.
You will find music there
Beyond the wildest imagination!

Gift Of The Black Mare

I enter your world now.
It is dark in the desert
Only the light of the stars
And half a moon
Crack through the sky.

To feel you I have to go into the dark
Pastures where I stumble
Not knowing where I can safely step.
Your eyes see more easily in the shadows.
You are familiar with this territory.
I have to trust you now.

You come towards me
Seeing me fully
In a way I do not know myself.
Your blue-black eyes mirror the light
Of the desert stars.
You look at me with a gaze so ancient
And familiar that I almost weep.

At once you touch my navel
With your nostrils,
The whiskers brushing finely
Against my bare skin
Calling me into present time.
Then you breathe onto my belly
Catching the scent of my life.

As you breathe in I feel that you
Have caught my umbilicus
Which has dangled since birth
And have attached it somewhere
Deep inside my soul.

Now your black face
Moves towards my chest.
Breathing out a stream of hot
Moist air, you invite my heart
To expand like the great wings
Of Pegasus.

Before you lose me in that dream,
You shift your breath to my eyes.
I must shut them to feel the gifts you bring me.

What I am left with
Is myself,
Entire and complete.
I am naked under the gaze
Of such a noble presence.
And I feel fully alive.

Peppertrees in Full Blossom

Have you heard the bees
In the late afternoon
By the Peppertrees in full blossom?
The horses stand in the shade
Flicking their tails
Relaxing into the hum
And vibration of the bees
Moving in and out of the flowers.
I never realized that they work within
Such an ecstatic rhythm.
It is an amazing love making.
The sound relaxes every nerve in this body
The mind is uplifted and the heart opens
Like a flower amongst the branches.
The sunlight sparks off the leaves
Silent cymbals adding to the orchestra of life.
Golden nectar of honey is already forming
In the collective gathering.
We are all participating
In performing our tasks.
All is well under the Peppertrees
And the horses are still
Flicking their tails.

The Windhorse

Last night the Windhorse came to visit me.
I thought he wanted to take me riding
Into the cosmos beyond time and space,

Instead he asked me to merge with him.
I felt a strong light which blinded my eyes
Temporarily my mind stopped its chatter
And I was filled with golden nectar
Overflowing from the Philosopher's Stone
Which had been my heart.
From my chest arose an illuminated Chalice
Overflowing with goodness.

I felt the love that God has for all things.
There are no exceptions
For the Infinite Light fills all of creation
With breath and awareness.
He breathes in and out
Bringing the natural world
Into form and then like an undercurrent
Of a vast ocean the tide draws us
Back into the formless.
He is like a mighty river
Immense and unstoppable.
Why be a stone when you too can flow
In the direction of life?

The Windhorse neighs.
It is time to roll out of him
Back into my bed of soft white blankets.
I thank him with a kiss.
Only now do I realize
His supreme strength.

He sniffs the currents
Reading the dimensions of time and space.
Then he is off into another dream
And I am left
In bliss.

About the Author

Ayn Cates Sullivan, MFA, Ph.D. holds degrees in literature from Hollins College, Columbia University and Kings College London, as well as a Masters from the University of Santa Monica Spiritual Psychology Program. She is the author of several books, a mother of two beautiful children who love rainbows and is married to her beloved, John Patrick Sullivan. She spent a decade in the United Kingdom seeking the Chalice, which she eventually discovered within her own heart. She lives in Ojai, California surrounded by eight horses who inspired the book.

Made in the USA
Lexington, KY
06 January 2013